Look at the picture and say what you see. A wizard waves a wand...

Fiddle deedee

Six rabbits in a row.
Three disappear...

GO GO GO

Eight rings on a string.
Three disappear...

Seven hats on a stand.
Three disappear...

Nine birds on a broom.
Three disappear...

Three wizards making a wish.
They disappear...

SWISH
SWISH
SWISH